SEX REASSIGNMENT SURGERY

WHAT ARE THE REASONS FOR SEX REASSIGNMENT

DR.PAGE KEMP

Contents

CHAPTER ONE

Sex REASSIGNMENT surgical treatment

Gender confirmation surgical procedure refers to processes that help human beings transition to their self-identified gender. Gender-affirming options might also consist of facial surgical remedy, pinnacle surgical operation or bottom surgical remedy. Most people who pick out gender affirmation surgeries report advanced intellectual fitness and best of life.

Sex reassignment surgical procedure refers to techniques that help people transition to their self-diagnosed gender. In recent times, many humans select to use the phrases gender confirmation or confirmation surgery.

Surgical approaches aren't required for gender confirmation, but many patients pick out to undergo one or greater surgical techniques. Communicate together with your health practitioner to speak about what surgical options can be right for you. The subsequent is an define of gender affirmation surgeries.

Penile production: This surgical operation can encompass elimination of the vagina (vaginectomy), reconstruction of the urethra and penile reconstruction. Surgeons may additionally additionally use each vaginal tissue or tissue from any other part of the frame to assemble the penis.

Phalloplasty is surgical operation for masculinizing gender confirmation.

Phalloplasty is a multistaged method that could embody a diffusion of strategies, collectively with:

Growing the penis

Lengthening the urethra so that you are capable of stand to urinate

Developing the pinnacle (glans) of the penis

Growing the scrotum

Casting off the vagina, uterus and ovaries

Setting erectile and testicular implants

Pores and pores and skin grafting from the donor tissue net page

Gender confirmation surgical treatment is customized to every character. Your surgical plan may additionally consist of greater or fewer of these steps and procedures.

Phalloplasty entails the usage of pores and skin flaps, which may be areas of skin moved from one place of the frame to some other. The skin flap is then reshaped, contoured and reattached to the groin to create the penis. There are three strategies the physician also can use to construct the penis, using pores and skin from the arm (radial forearm loose flap), leg (anterolateral thigh flap) or aspect (latissimus dorsi flap).

There are specialists and cons to every method. Factors for deciding on pores and skin flap locations consist of the affected person's health and fat distribution, nerve function, blood flow and favored surgical results.

What is a radial forearm free flap?

A radial forearm free flap (RFFF) includes taking the pores and pores and skin, fat, nerves, arteries and veins out of your wrist to approximately midway up your forearm to create the penis. Usually, the scientific professional will use your nondominant hand so it is easier as a way to get better and go again on your everyday sports activities.

Throughout your surgical session, the doctor will take a look at the blood glide on your arm and hand noninvasively. This includes briefly putting pressure on arteries then releasing the stress to test blood distribution inside the arm and hand.

There are 3 stages to this system.

Level 1: the first degree of an RFFF approach is growing the penis the usage of tissue from the forearm. The region wherein the forearm tissue is taken might require a pores and skin graft. This can arise at the time of the preliminary phalloplasty surgical operation, or it is able to occur three to 5 weeks in a while. If it takes region later, patients can have a transient skin masking over the forearm to help it heal.

Degree 2: the second one degree, scheduled about 5 to 6 months later, also can encompass lengthening the urethra to allow for urination out of the top of the penis, developing the scrotum and removing the vagina, and other strategies counting on the affected person's individualized plan.

Stage 3: The third degree of surgery involves putting in region testicle implants and an erectile tool to help the affected individual gain an erection. The 1/3 level usually takes location one year after the second.

Will i have a say in how the phalloplasty is staged and the surgical plan?

Your gender affirmation surgical procedure is particularly customized. Relying on what's most vital to you, your surgical treatment group will paintings with you on a custom designed plan ahead. You and your physician will talk your priorities and decide which approaches are proper for you. Each degree may be scheduled to make certain your fitness and safety and provide the first-rate danger of proper outcomes.

How prolonged will I be in the sanatorium?

After your diploma 1 surgical procedure, you'll stay as an inpatient for four to five days. Your surgical group will often display the blood supply to the tissue that has been used to create your new penis and make certain you are capable of use the rest room and stroll round after surgical operation. Techniques for levels 2 and 3 do not require a medical institution stay.

Will I want a catheter?

For the duration of your inpatient live for degree 1 surgical treatment, you could have a suprapubic tube that is going at once into your bladder and a few different catheter in your local urethra for at least five days. It is usually eliminated inside the sanatorium earlier than you pass home.

If you make a decision now not to have urethral lengthening as part of diploma 2, you will have a Foley catheter positioned in the working room and eliminated earlier than you leave the medical institution. If you make a decision to have urethral lengthening, you will skip domestic with a Foley catheter within the new urethra and a suprapubic tube. A clamp guarantees that the urethra does no longer leak urine.

What is a suprapubic tube?

A suprapubic tube (SPT) permits urine to empty from your bladder. It's far located in the decrease part of your stomach, underneath the stomach button. The SPT stays in for 4 to 5 weeks, depending for your restoration and restoration.

When will my SPT be removed?

In advance than the SPT is eliminated, spherical 4 weeks after surgical remedy, a urologist will carry out a retrograde urethrogram. This consists of putting dye into the bladder via the brand new urethra. An X-ray tracks the dye to see if the brand new urethra is open and equipped for urination. If so, the doctor will clamp the

SPT and you may be allowed to urinate from your new urethra. If the whole lot appears first-rate after a few days, the SPT is eliminated.

Different pores and skin Flaps utilized in Phalloplasty

What is an anterolateral thigh flap?

An anterolateral thigh flap (ALT) uses pores and skin, fats, nerves, arteries and veins from the leg to create a penis. A completely unique vascular CT test can assist the health care professional have a look at the blood deliver of every leg to determine which leg will be higher for growing the pores and skin flap.

The degree of the ALT phalloplasty are much

like the RFFF. The vicinity wherein the thigh tissue is taken may even require a skin graft. The ensuing scar at the thigh can be protected with shorts.

What's a musculocutaneous latissimus dorsi flap?

A musculocutaneous latissimus dorsi pores and skin flap (MLD) consists of the pores and skin, fats, nerves, arteries and veins from the facet of your decrease lower back to create a penis. The overall practitioner may additionally order a special CT test to test the blood float for the duration of the donor internet site vicinity.

The tiers of the MLD phalloplasty are similar to the RFFF and ALT. But, the vicinity from which the decrease lower back tissue is taken generally does now not require a pores and skin graft and can be closed in a straight line. The scar may be protected with a shirt. Sufferers can also enjoy some initial weak spot raising their arm, however this improves with time.

How is penis size determined?

Penis length relies upon on affected individual possibilities and the skin flap harvested from your frame. Thinner sufferers with less fat at the pores and pores and skin flap can have a penis with much less girth. As an alternative, sufferers with a more quantity of fat could have a thicker penis.

CHAPTER TWO

The length of the penis is predicated upon at the affected character's donor internet site, however commonly it's far approximately five–6 inches. After the primary degree, the penis may lower in size as postoperative swelling decreases and the tissue settles into its new vicinity.

What determines scrotum length?

Scrotum period is particular to the affected individual and is based upon on the amount of pores and skin that is gift inside the genital vicinity earlier than phalloplasty. The greater genital tissue there is, the bigger the scrotum and the testicular implants may be.

There are exclusive approaches to create the scrotum, which encompass a technique referred to as V-Y scrotoplasty, a way that creates a pouch to preserve testicular implants. AART silicone round carving blocks have been approved with the resource of the Strategies to talk approximately together with your medical medical doctor earlier than Phalloplasty

Every individual present procedure gender affirmation surgical remedy is unique. Your preferred practitioner will artwork with you to speak about which processes, and their timing, are fine for you and your goals.

Have to i have a hysterectomy earlier than phalloplasty surgical treatment?

For the ones inquisitive about this method,

hysterectomies are normally accomplished earlier than phalloplasty and do no longer require a vaginectomy.

Urethral Lengthening before Phalloplasty

In case you select out to have urethral lengthening, this method consists of lengthening your existing urethra so you are able to urinate out of the end of the penis. It involves connecting your contemporary urethra to the present day urethra created inside the shaft of the penis.

Now not all patients choose to have urethral lengthening; however, this could be a vital step if you want to stand whilst you urinate. It's also essential to recognise that if making a decision not to have urethral lengthening in level 1 of your phalloplasty, it's going to not be feasible to have the lengthening process later.

Complications of Urethral Lengthening

The maximum not unusual headaches for urethral lengthening encompass urethral strictures (narrowed regions of the urethra), fistula (advent of a passageway between the urethra and every other place) and diverticula (formation of a pouch inside the urethra). This could require a further surgical treatment to restore.

What is a metoidioplasty?

A metoidioplasty is a surgical operation to attain masculine-performing genitalia with fewer steps than a phalloplasty. The pores and skin of the labia and across the clitoris is lengthened to obtain the appearance of a penis. Some humans prefer to undergo a metoidioplasty in the event that they do no longer need to use tissue from their palms or legs to create a penis or inside the occasion that they determine upon a shorter, greater trustworthy surgical procedure.

A metoidioplasty manner has a quicker healing and much less headaches. Surgeons can discuss metoidioplasty with patients and assist them decide if this option is proper for them.

Will I need to have hair removal?

Yes, before surgical treatment, when you are searching for advice from the surgical group and pick a pores and skin flap website, you could get a template for hair removal that you can supply on your hair removal expert.

What if i have a tattoo on my favored donor site?

So long as there is right blood waft and nerve function, donor web sites — even people with a tattoo — may be used.

Penile function and Sensation After Phalloplasty

What am i able to do with a reconstructed penis?

Penis feature is decided via manner of what you and your surgical operation institution agree on on your surgical plan. If it's far crucial so that you can urinate out of the give up of your penis, then urethral lengthening can be a tremendous desire for you. If sensation is most critical, your group will attention on a donor internet website online with proper nerve innervation. If penetrative sex is maximum essential, and also you would love to hold an erection, then implanting an erectile prosthetic can be a part of your surgical operation plan.

Can i get an erection after phalloplasty?

In degree three phalloplasty, a urologist can vicinity a prosthetic erectile device a terrific manner to will let you preserve an erection. As of September 2022, no implantable prosthetic devices have been FDA-accepted for phalloplasty. As an alternative, the health care professional can use a device meant for sufferers with erectile dysfunction to permit transmasculine patients to reap an erection. There's a chance of contamination and implant rejection with an erectile implant. If this takes place, it may take six months earlier than every other tool may be located into the penis.

What shape of sensation and feeling am i capable of expect?

Sensation healing varies with the resource of affected character. Nerve regeneration can begin as early as three weeks after surgery, but it may take longer in a few patients. Every so often sensation can absorb to a 12 months or longer. Go returned of nerve sensation isn't confident. As nerves regenerate and supply a lift to connections, you would possibly revel in taking pix ache, tingling or electric sensations. As time is going on, the tingling feeling starts offevolved to subside.

<h3 style="text-align:center">What is nerve hookup during phalloplasty?</h3>

Nerve hookup consists of taking gift nerves from the donor website, at the side of the arm, and connecting them to nerves positioned in the pelvis. This lets in you to have sensation within the reconstructed penis.

<h3 style="text-align:center">What's clitoral burying at some point of phalloplasty surgery?</h3>

Clitoral burying consists of shifting the clitoris into the base of the penis to increase sensation. This is generally done at level 2.

Is orgasm possible after phalloplasty?

Orgasm is feasible after phalloplasty, specially in case your surgical treatment plan emphasizes maintaining sensation. It is vital to observe that your penis will no longer ejaculate with semen at the time of orgasm.

Vaginal creation (vaginoplasty): ☐ This surgical procedure is a multistage device throughout which surgeons may get rid of the penis (penectomy) and the testes (orchiectomy), if however present, and use tissues from the penis to assemble the vagina, the clitoris (clitoroplasty) and the labia (labiaplasty).

What is vaginoplasty?

Vaginoplasty is surgical treatment to create a vagina. It consists of doing away with the penis, testicles and scrotum.

Vaginoplasty involves rearranging tissue in the genital vicinity to create a vaginal canal (or starting) and vulva (external genitalia), together with the labia. To create the vaginal canal, the health care company uses a mixture of the pores and skin surrounding the triumphing penis together with the scrotal pores and skin. Depending on how an entire lot skin is available in the genital area, the general practitioner may additionally additionally need to apply a pores and skin graft from the stomach or thigh to assemble a complete vaginal canal.

Vaginoplasty is mostly a one-degree gadget. A few patients have their testicles eliminated (orchiectomy) earlier than vaginoplasty, but this isn't required. In reality, having the orchiectomy before your vaginoplasty can growth the danger of wanting pores and pores and skin grafts.

Do I need to have hair removal before vaginoplasty? Even as should I begin?

Sure, you may want to have eternal hair elimination in advance than surgical treatment. The surgical group will provide you with a template in the course of your session for the regions that require hair removal. Sufferers are recommended to start hair removal as quick as possible, for the reason that it is able to take three to 6 months to finish the method.

Will I want any extra surgical procedure after vaginoplasty?

You could want extra surgical tactics to revise the advent of the new vagina and vulva. Later revisions can improve aesthetic look, however those are not typically protected with the aid of insurance.

From time to time, patients revel in complications associated with vaginoplasty. These can consist of narrowing of the vaginal canal or a fistula (an abnormal connection among the brand new vagina and the rectum or bladder). The ones complications are usually handled with some different surgical operation.

How lengthy is vaginoplasty surgical treatment?

Most surgical procedures remaining among seven and 10 hours.

Recuperation After Vaginoplasty

After surgery, you'll be admitted to the medical institution for about five or six days. You'll spend most of this time in bed improving. As you get towards discharge, you could begin sitting and walking round. Your care team will monitor your ache, and ensure you're recuperation because it have to be and capable of go to the bathroom and stroll.

On average, it may take six to eight weeks to recover from a vaginoplasty. Each affected character's healing is exceptional, but proper home hygiene and postoperative care will come up with the awesome danger for a quicker recovery.

Will i have a catheter?

Even as you are within the hospital, you could have a Foley catheter inside the urethra so that it will be taken out earlier than you pass domestic.

Will i've surgical drains?

Positive, your health care provider will region a drain on the identical time as you are within the jogging room, with a purpose to be removed in advance than you leave.

CHAPTER THREE

What form of hygiene is needed after vaginoplasty?

Beginning eight days after surgical remedy, you'll begin douching (cleansing the vaginal canal). While douching, you need to use a nonscented vaginal douche. You have to douche at the least as soon as in keeping with week, counting on the amount of vaginal discharge you are experiencing. If you observe you're having plenty of vaginal discharge, you can boom your douching time table.

It's also very vital to hold the external genital location dry. If the area is looking very pink and moist, such as you have been soaking in a tub too lengthy, you may place an absorbent pad most of the outer lips (labia) to wick away greater moisture.

Am i able to bathe after vaginoplasty surgical procedure?

Sure. It is very essential to easy the area to save you infections. You can lightly wash the region with cleaning soap and water. In no manner scrub or permit water to be sprayed immediately on the surgical website on-line.

Goes to the relaxation room one-of-a-type?

It is vital to recall for the rest of your lifestyles that once wiping with relaxation room paper or washing the genital area, continuously wipe front to returned. This enables preserve your vagina easy and stops infection from the anal place.

You'll be aware a few spraying even as you urinate. That is common and may be addressed with physical treatment to assist give a boost to the pelvic ground. A physical therapist can help you with physical games, which may additionally moreover help enhance urination over the years.

Is the vagina created by using the usage of vaginoplasty sexually practical?

Positive. You need to keep away from any shape of sexual hobby for 12 weeks after surgical operation. Sexual hobby for the duration of your restoration length can delay wound recuperation and motive headaches.

Twelve weeks after surgical remedy, the vagina may be used for receptive sex. Moreover, the clitoris might also have sensation.

How prolonged does it take for sensation to come lower back?

Sensation is not confident after vaginoplasty, however it is essential to keep in mind that this detail of healing is special for each affected person gift procedure this technique. Nerve feature can return as early as 3 weeks after surgical operation. Once in a while this way takes a 12 months or longer.

What is the commonplace depth of a vagina after vaginoplasty?

The depth is based upon on affected man or woman opportunities and anatomy. On common, the built vaginal canal is among 4 and 6 inches deep. Vaginal depth is dependent on the amount of pores and skin to be had within the genital region before your vaginoplasty. This varies amongst people, and some sufferers can also need pores and pores and skin grafts. A few sufferers can also request a no-intensity or minimum-depth vaginal canal, which is likewise possible.

What is dilation after vaginoplasty?

A part of the recuperation method after vaginoplasty involves dilation — setting a medical grade dilator into the vagina to keep your vaginal canal open because it heals.

The hospital may additionally additionally offer you with a set of numerous sized dilators to use.

A medical doctor or therapist out of your care group will show you a way to dilate. This may be hard at the start, however specialists will paintings with you and your consolation degree to help you get aware of this element of your healing gadget. You could begin dilating with the smallest dilator inside the dilator percentage. You still use this dilator until cleared to enhance to the subsequent length via using your care team.

Sooner or later of the first few weeks after surgical treatment, you should dilate two instances a day for as a minimum 15 minutes. It is very critical that you maintain dilating, specially at some stage in your immediately postoperative period, to save you dropping vaginal intensity and width. Sufferers keep to apply a dilator for so long as the care organization recommends. Some patients may additionally need to dilate their entire lives.

Is dilation after vaginoplasty painful?

Dilation want to no longer be a painful gadget. Inside the starting, you could experience pain as you studies the perfect angles and techniques in your frame. In case you feel intense ache at any time for the duration of dilation, it's far important to forestall, alter the dilator, and reposition your frame so you are more comfy. It's also crucial to apply lubricant even as you dilate.

A pelvic ground therapist can work with you that will help you get used to this element of healing.

Pinnacle surgery is surgical procedure that receives rid of or augments breast tissue and reshapes the chest to create a greater masculine or female look for transgender and nonbinary humans.

What's top surgical remedy?

Pinnacle surgical procedure is every other call for chest masculinization or feminization. Using considered one in all several surgical methods, surgeons increase or do away with breast tissue, and in some cases reshape and reposition the nipples for an affirming appearance.

Who might also benefit from pinnacle surgical remedy?

Transgender and nonbinary people may also choose top surgical remedy as a part of their gender affirmation remedy. Gender affirmation surgical operation can deal with gender dysphoria, which takes place while gender identification does now not correspond to intercourse assigned at starting.

Gender affirmation surgical procedure can enhance nicely-being in patients who:

Have ongoing and documented gender dysphoria.

Have the prison and mental potential to make responsible scientific choices for themselves.

Are efficaciously addressing special intellectual and physical fitness issues.

At the identical time as testosterone remedy isn't always required for chest masculinization surgery, some surgeons and insurance organizations will request three hundred and sixty five days of estrogen remedy to maximize natural breast boom previous to implant placement.

Styles of pinnacle surgical remedy

Depending at the affected person's desires, the physician may additionally additionally propose numerous specific techniques for pinnacle surgical remedy:

For chest feminization:

Breast augmentation with implants.

Breast augmentation with fats grafting.

Breast augmentation with implants and fat grafting.

For chest masculinization:

Dispose of breast tissue and overlying pores and skin.

Get rid of the crease along the lowest of the breast (the inframammary crease).

Contour the chest and emphasize the pectoral muscle tissues.

Make the nipples and areolas smaller and reposition them (nipple grafts).

Eliminate the nipples totally relying on patient alternatives.

You and your physician will speak the exceptional choice for you, based in your body kind, fitness, goals and exceptional elements.

Breast cancer chance

Removal of breast tissue does no longer completely dispose of the threat of breast cancer developing inside the region. In case you are at threat for inherited breast most cancers, make certain to inform your medical doctor. A few care carriers recommend a baseline mammogram before your pinnacle surgery procedures. You may nevertheless require tracking for breast maximum cancers even after putting off breast tissue.

CHAPTER FOUR

Estrogen can increase breast most cancers chance. The ones on estrogen treatment may also experience breast increase as a result. A few physicians or care carriers might also moreover recommend a baseline mammogram previous to chest feminization and breast cancer tracking after chest feminization.

Double Incision approach for Chest Masculinization

That is the maximum commonplace system for pinnacle surgical treatment, and may remove mild to huge amounts of breast tissue. Incisions are made horizontally, throughout the left and proper side of your chest, which intensify the natural contours of the pectoral muscle mass. The greater the quantity of tissue gift earlier than the surgical procedure, the bigger the incisions. Your nipples and areolas are removed, resized, reshaped, and then replaced (if preferred) to gain a more masculine appearance.

Keyhole top surgical remedy for Chest Masculinization

For humans with very small quantities of breast tissue and firm pores and skin, the doctor should make a reduce alongside the lower half of the areola and extract breast tissue via this starting. The areola and nipple can be decreased in size in advance than ultimate the incision.

Top surgical procedure: What happens

Your manner will normally take three to 5 hours.

Top surgical procedure techniques are completed as outpatient surgical procedure. This means that that most sufferers will not be admitted to the health facility.

The health care expert will mark the region for surgical treatment for your chest at the same time as you are sitting upright. The marks help ensure your surgical remedy consequences are as symmetrical and natural looking as feasible.

You'll be given anesthesia thru an IV that will help you sleep thru the method.

You may be located to your returned on a

table with padding round your arms to make certain you live still and secure.

You may awaken from the technique with stitches and dressings in your chest. If you received chest masculinization, you'll also have a chest binder. In case you received chest feminization, you will certainly have a surgical bra.

Getting better from top surgical procedure

It is very crucial to comply with all the instructions your surgical operation crew gives you even as you flow home from the hospital. For several weeks after surgical treatment you need to no longer raise your fingers greater than ninety ranges a long way out of your frame or over your head.

You need to also no longer push, pull or increase some thing more than 5 pounds at some point of those 4 weeks. This ensures your scar will heal properly and now not stretch and become large.

Pain. You could revel in a few pain for a few days after surgery, however commonly after 4 to 5 days your pain will ease and can be controlled with over-the-counter acetaminophen and ibuprofen.

Dressings and drains. You will have dressings and probable drains in region while you go away the medical institution. Do no longer eliminate them until you notice your medical health practitioner after surgical operation. If you have drains, your health practitioner's workplace will provide you with commands on a way to empty them. Those drains assist save you fluid from collecting inside the chest or breast. Please document the quantity of fluid coming out of the drains. Your drains will normally be eliminated at your first appointment after surgical treatment.

Bathing and showering. Till you observe the physician, you may bathe your lower frame if you could accomplish that without getting the bandages and dressings wet. Smooth the top of your body with a sponge simplest till your medical health practitioner offers you the go-beforehand for showering and bathing.

Compression garment. After chest masculinization surgical treatment, you could put on a compression vest. This vest is positioned to your frame inside the jogging room after surgical remedy. It is very crucial to place at the vest at all times to save you submit-operative bleeding and fluid collections.

Surgical bra. After chest feminization surgical remedy you will wear a surgical bra. This is a unique bra located to your body within the strolling room after surgical treatment. It is very critical to wear the bra at all times to prevent postoperative bleeding and fluid collections.

Dangers, headaches and side outcomes of pinnacle surgical remedy

Pinnacle surgical procedure scars: For chest masculinization strategies, scars may additionally seem as horizontal traces in the course of the chest, or circles across the areolas. For chest feminization strategies, the scars can be positioned beneath the breasts. It could take in to 18 months for scars to treatment, and a few people determine directly to have similarly surgery to decrease them. It's far critical to keep away from sun exposure, which can darken scars and make them more apparent.

Hematoma: Blood can gather inside the tissues after surgical procedure and shape a clot, with signs and signs which encompass ache, swelling and discoloration in addition to an elevated risk for infection. Hematomas shape in approximately 1% to 2% of pinnacle surgical processes.

Seroma: Fluid can collect below the pores and skin. Small seromas may not need any treatment and depart on their personal. Seromas in pinnacle surgical operation can be avoided through drains within the surgical area and carrying your compression vest usually after your manner.

Contamination: this is a unprecedented problem of top surgery, but can appear. Cellulitis within the surgical location may also require remedy with oral antibiotics and drainage.

Breakdown of nipple graft: while a few pores and skin sloughing is not any cause for problem, deeper tissue demise (necrosis) can indicate that the graft isn't always a fulfillment and greater surgical operation may be crucial.

Decreased nipple sensitivity: Numbness or tingling can take place if a nerve is disrupted or damaged in the direction of surgical treatment. The double incision technique for chest masculinization involves eliminating and repositioning the nipple, which calls for decreasing the nerves. Nipple numbness also can decorate over time, but full recuperation of sensation is not going.

Irregular contours: extra surgical remedy to address chest contour can be known as for in as much as 32% of top methods.

Facial gender surgical remedy: at the identical time as hormone substitute therapy can assist attain gender placing forward changes to the face, surgical operation can also help.

Facial gender surgical treatment can embody a ramification of techniques to create greater feminine abilties, like reshaping the nostril; brow bring (or brow elevate); chin, cheek and jaw reshaping; Adam's apple cut price; lip augmentation; hairline healing; and earlobe discount.

Facial gender surgical operation can also encompass a series of strategies to create greater masculine capabilities, collectively with forehead lengthening and augmentation; cheek augmentation; reshaping the nostril and chin; jaw augmentation; and thyroid cartilage enhancement to construct an Adam's apple.

Hysterectomy: This surgical treatment includes the elimination of the uterus and ovaries (oophorectomy). There are options for oocyte storage and fertility protection that you can need to speak about along side your doctor.

Hysterectomy is surgical operation to do away with the uterus. After a hysterectomy, you'll now not menstruate (have periods) or be able to get pregnant. Uterus removal is a commonplace remedy for a variety of conditions that affect a female's reproductive organs.

Approximately 1/2 of one million hysterectomies are finished each year inside the U.S. It's miles the second one maximum commonplace surgical operation for girls, after cesarean transport (C-segment). Maximum hysterectomies are carried out many of the a while of forty and 50.

What is a hysterectomy?

A hysterectomy eliminates the uterus and the connected cervix. The shape of hysterectomy you have got will rely upon the motive for treatment.

Styles of Hysterectomies

There are various varieties of hysterectomies. Your medical doctor will speak the risks, benefits and capacity side results of each technique. It's critical to invite your physician if elimination of the ovaries and fallopian tubes at some point of your hysterectomy is usually recommended.

Styles of hysterectomies include:

General hysterectomy removes the complete uterus and the cervix (most commonplace kind).

Partial hysterectomy (moreover known as supracervical hysterectomy) removes simplest the uterus, leaving in the back of the cervix (studies is ongoing about the risks and advantages of leaving the cervix intact).

Radical hysterectomy removes the uterus, cervix and pinnacle part of the vagina (generally for cancer treatment).

How prolonged does hysterectomy surgical operation take?

Hysterectomy surgical remedy can take between one and 4 hours. The period of surgical procedure relies upon on the shape of device you've got and the way it's miles executed.

Reasons for a Hysterectomy

There are a selection of motives your medical doctor can also additionally advise a hysterectomy, which includes:

Ordinary bleeding

Adenomyosis

Dysmenorrhea (painful menses)

Endometriosis

Gynecologic cancers, including maximum cancers of the uterus, ovary, cervix or endometrium

Heavy or prolonged menstrual bleeding (menorrhagia)

Fibroids

Uterine prolapse, which may be combined with bladder restore

Gender affirmation for men who are transgender and people who are nonbinary

Belly Hysterectomy

A health practitioner plays an stomach, or open, hysterectomy thru an incision (reduce) in your belly. The incision can be horizontal and occasional for your stomach, really above your pubic bone, or vertical extending as much as or beyond the belly button, relying on the indication for surgical procedure and the dimensions of the pathology.

CHAPTER FIVE

Anesthesia: sizable

Hospitalization: to a few days

Incision size: six to twelve inches for horizontal incisions; longer for vertical incisions

Method time: one to four hours

Restoration: six to twelve weeks, relying on the incision length and sort

Laparoscopic or robot Hysterectomy

In lots of times, a hysterectomy may be finished the use of minimally invasive techniques. A laparoscopic hysterectomy is completed through severa small incisions on your stomach in place of one huge incision.

A medical doctor inserts an endoscope (a thin video digital camera) thru one incision. The laparoscope permits the doctor to view your pelvic organs on a video monitor. The stomach is distended with gasoline to create a location to feature in. Small surgical tools are used in the unique incisions to put off your uterus intact or in sections.

A robot hysterectomy is a few other form of minimally invasive uterus removal. Your healthcare professional makes use of the help of a robotic tool to remove your uterus thru small abdominal incisions.

Anesthesia: standard

Hospitalization: none (outpatient) or one night

Incision period: 5–12 millimeters

Method time: one to four hours

Recovery: to six weeks

Hysteroscopic Hysterectomy

Hysteroscopic (vaginal) hysterectomy is the least invasive technique to uterus elimination. The uterus is eliminated thru an incision on the pinnacle of the vagina, so you don't have any stomach incisions.

Several factors may also determine whether or not you are a candidate for a vaginal hysterectomy, such as situations that could save you vaginal get proper of access to to the uterus, which include lack of uterine descent, immoderate endometriosis, uterine fibroid, need to remove the ovaries and/or fallopian tubes, adhesions (scar tissue) or medical doctor desire/enjoy.

For a vaginal hysterectomy, you could count on:

Anesthesia: popular

Hospitalization: one or nights

Incision size: none

Manner time: one to four hours

Recuperation: 3 to four weeks

Hysterectomy side outcomes and dangers

Hysterectomy is generally a cozy procedure with amazing achievement expenses. However, ability risks and side outcomes of the process encompass:

Early menopause, with symptoms which consist of warm flashes, temper swings or insomnia if ovaries are removed

Excessive bleeding and need for blood transfusion

Ability damage to adjoining organs inclusive of the bladder, intestines, ureters, blood vessels and nerves

Blood clots to legs or lungs

Scar tissue formation

Hernia

Ache

Reactions to anesthesia

Contamination

Hysterectomy restoration

After a hysterectomy, keep away from strenuous hobby, intercourse and lifting heavy items. Your doctor will allow you to realize even as you may resume normal sports together with paintings, workout and sexual intercourse.

Hysterectomy for Gender affirmation

Men who're transgender and people who're nonbinary can also keep in mind hysterectomy, salpingectomy (removal of the fallopian tubes), oophorectomy (elimination of the ovaries) or a mixture of those procedures as part of their gender affirmation surgical remedy plan.

The manner or methods you and your medical doctor decide on can also depend upon several elements. These may additionally additionally include your ultra-modern health and your alternatives regarding fertility and the potential to hold a being pregnant or to come to be a natural decide. Reproductive technology experts can provide an cause of your alternatives, inclusive of egg freezing and different ways to preserve fertility.

Orchiectomy is surgical treatment to eliminate one or each of the testicles, the 2 oval glands inside the sac referred to as the scrotum. Bilateral orchiectomy — eliminating each testicles — may be a part of gender confirmation remedy for girls who are transgender and people who are nonbinary.

A few human beings might also integrate this way with a scrotectomy, it truly is surgical treatment to get rid of all or part of the scrotum. For others, the pores and pores and skin of the scrotum can be utilized in vulvoplasty or vaginoplasty — the surgical creation of a vulva or vagina.

The gadget reduces testosterone

manufacturing and may dispose of the want for continuing treatment with estrogen and androgen-suppressing medicinal pills. Your fitness care practitioner will talk alternatives which consist of sperm freezing earlier than orchiectomy which could preserve your functionality to come to be a biological figure.

Recovery After Gender affirmation surgeries

Recovery time from a gender affirmation surgical procedure or system varies, relying on the machine. Speak to your physician approximately what you can anticipate.

THE END